MINNESOTA

The Land of 10,000 Lakes

Rachel Keranen, Marlene Brill, and
Elizabeth Kaplan

Cavendish
Square

New York

Published in 2019 by Cavendish Square Publishing, LLC
243 5th Avenue, Suite 136, New York, NY 10016

Library of Congress Cataloging-in-Publication Data

Names: Keranen, Rachel, author. | Brill, Marlene Targ, author. | Kaplan,
Elizabeth, 1956- author.
Title: Minnesota / Rachel Keranen, Marlene Targ Brill, and Elizabeth Kaplan.
Description: New York : Cavendish Square, 2019. | Series: It's my state! (fourth edition)
Includes bibliographical references and index. | Audience: Grades 3-5.
Identifiers: LCCN 2017049408 (print) | LCCN 2017051079 (ebook) | ISBN 9781502626295
(library bound) | ISBN 9781502626172 (ebook) | ISBN 9781502644459 (pbk.)
Subjects: LCSH: Minnesota--Juvenile literature.
Classification: LCC F606.3 (ebook) | LCC F606.3 .B75 2019 (print) | DDC
977.6--dc23
LC record available at https://lccn.loc.gov/2017049408

Editorial Director: David McNamara
Editor: Caitlyn Miller
Copy Editor: Nathan Heidelberger
Associate Art Director: Alan Sliwinski
Designer: Jessica Nevins
Production Coordinator: Karol Szymczuk
Photo Research: J8 Media

It's My
STATE!

Table of Contents

SNAPSHOT
MINNESOTA

The Land of 10,000 Lakes

Statehood
May 11, 1858

Population
5,576,606
(2017 census estimate)

Capital
Saint Paul

State Flag

The Minnesota state flag shows a version of the state seal surrounded by stars. The top star is the largest and represents the North Star. The seal is surrounded by pink and white lady's slippers, and the stars surround the seal and the slippers. The date 1819 represents the founding of Fort Snelling, 1858 is the year of statehood, and 1893 represents the adoption of the first state flag.

State Song

"Hail! Minnesota"
The song is a slow ballad that originated as the school song of the University of Minnesota. It was composed in 1904 by Truman Rickard. In 1945, the Minnesota State **Legislature** named "Hail! Minnesota" the state song.

HISTORICAL EVENTS TIMELINE

1679
A French explorer named Daniel Greysolon, sieur Du Lhut, claims the Upper Mississippi region for France.

1763
At the end of the French and Indian War, France gives England all French territory east of the Mississippi River (except New Orleans), including part of Minnesota.

1858
Minnesota becomes the thirty-second state.

State Seal

The state seal shows a barefoot farmer plowing a field near Saint Anthony Falls on the Mississippi River. The farmer represents the agriculture of the state. His axe, gun, and powder horn rest on a stump, which represents the state's timber industry. Nearby, a Native American man rides a horse. He holds a spear that represents hunting. The banner bears the state motto, "L'Etoile du Nord." The motto is written in French. In English, it translates to "The Star of the North." In the distance, the sun sets over the plains. The three pine trees represent the three major pine regions in Minnesota.

State Tree

Red Pine

Minnesota's red pines are commonly found in the northern and northeastern parts of the state. As the trees age, the bark turns reddish brown, giving the tree its name. Minnesota's tallest red pine is 120 feet (37 meters) tall and more than three hundred years old. The tree is also called the Norway pine in Minnesota, though they don't actually grow in Norway.

State Flower

Pink and White Lady's Slipper

Minnesota's wetlands, bogs, and forests are home to lady's slippers. The flowers are pink and white and are shaped like moccasins. The bright orchids grow slowly and can live for up to one hundred years. Their name comes from an Ojibwa legend. The legend tells of a young girl who journeyed to find medicine for her village, losing her slippers in the snow along the way.

1862	1889	1905
The US-Dakota War breaks out in Minnesota. It lasts for six weeks. The Dakota surrender and are forced to leave Minnesota.	The world-famous Mayo Clinic is founded in Rochester by Charles Horace Mayo and William Worrall Mayo.	Twenty-nine ships are damaged or destroyed in a terrible storm on Lake Superior, called the Mataafa Storm. A total of thirty-nine people die in the storm.

State Drink
Milk

State Gemstone
Lake Superior Agate

State Muffin
Blueberry

1975	1978	1985
The first Hmong family resettles in Minnesota from Asia. By 2010, the Twin Cities are home to the largest urban Hmong population in the country.	The Boundary Waters Canoe Area Wilderness Act designates 1,098,057 acres (444,368 hectares) of land as protected.	Minnesota musician Prince Rogers Nelson, best known as Prince, wins three Grammy Awards.

State Mushroom
Morel

State Bird
Common Loon

CURRENT EVENTS TIMELINE

1998

Professional wrestler Jesse Ventura is elected governor of Minnesota.

2007

The I-35 W bridge collapses over the Mississippi River during evening rush hour, killing 13 people and injuring 145.

2017

Minnesota's largest measles outbreak in thirty years comes to an end. A downturn in vaccinations allowed the outbreak to spread.

The Saint Louis River feeds into Lake Superior. Minnesota is known for its lakes and waterways.

1 Geography

"Minnesota" is a Dakota word meaning "sky-blue waters." The name describes a key element of Minnesota's geography: its lakes and rivers. Though Minnesota is sometimes called "the land of 10,000 lakes," the nickname is as modest as its people. Minnesota actually has 11,842 lakes that are 10 acres (4 hectares) or greater in size. The state contains the origin of the Mississippi River, the second-longest river in North America. Minnesota also boasts the western shore of the largest freshwater lake in the world by surface area, Lake Superior. The state's lakes have more total shoreline (44,926 miles, or 72,301 kilometers) than the combined lake and coastal shorelines of California (about 35,427 miles, or 57,014 km).

Minnesota is also blanketed with forests and prairies. Its different terrains, plus a wide range of weather from north to south, make Minnesota seem like several states in one. It is the twelfth-largest state, with a land area of 79,610 square miles (206,189 square kilometers) plus 7,329 square miles (18,982 sq km) of water area.

The state's lakes and rivers have a fascinating origin. Minnesota has been covered by glaciers (huge sheets of slow-moving ice) many times. The most recent glacier period began about

Minnesota borders Canada, as well as the US states of Wisconsin, Iowa, North Dakota, and South Dakota.

seventy-five thousand years ago and ended about ten thousand years ago. As the glaciers moved in, they flattened hills and dug out valleys. As they moved out, they deposited soil, sand, and rocks and left behind blocks of ice. Lakes formed when the ice melted. Rivers formed as the melting ice drained away.

Minnesota can be divided into four geographic regions, based on the main **ecosystem** in each region. The northeastern and north-central portion of the state is covered in coniferous forests. These forests consist of needled trees like pines, spruces, firs, and tamaracks. The southeastern corner of the state and a diagonal swath northwest toward the state's center are covered in deciduous forests. They are made of trees that lose their leaves each fall. The western border and southwestern corner of the state are composed of prairie grassland. Most of the prairie has been turned into farmland. However, some remnants of the gently rolling grasslands remain. A small section in the northwest of the state is covered in tallgrass aspen parkland. This is a mixture of prairie grasses, flowers, and deciduous trees.

Eagle Mountain is the highest point in the state.

Coniferous Forests

Coniferous forests of pine, spruce, and fir trees mixed with deciduous pine, aspen, and birch trees blanket northeastern Minnesota. This area of the state is shaped like an arrowhead, with Canada to the north and Lake Superior to the south and east. It is the snowiest part of the state. The area is also sometimes called the Superior Uplands. Minnesota's tallest peak, Eagle Mountain, is located here. It rises 2,301 feet (701 meters) above sea level.

The North Shore of Lake Superior makes up 150 miles (241 km) of the area's varied shoreline.

Boaters on the beautiful lake can see waterfalls tumbling down cliffs some 1,000 feet (300 m) high. Through the port of Duluth on Lake Superior, Minnesota is connected to the other four Great Lakes, to the Saint Lawrence River, and finally to the Atlantic Ocean.

Duluth boasts an important port.

The Arrowhead is famous for its Boundary Waters Canoe Area Wilderness, which straddles the border with Canada. Here, more than 1,100 lakes and streams cut through lush forests. People can travel for hours in nonmotorized boats, stopping to fish or simply to enjoy the area's peaceful beauty. The Arrowhead also includes the Superior National Forest.

Northern Minnesota includes the northernmost point in the United States outside Alaska. This "point" is actually within a huge lake called Lake of the Woods. Because of Minnesota's border agreements, a small part of land along the northwestern side of Lake of the Woods belongs to Minnesota but is surrounded by Canadian land. The area is called the Northwest Angle and contains the northernmost town in the lower forty-eight states: Angle Inlet. To reach Angle Inlet by road, Minnesotans have to travel through Manitoba, Canada. Passing through customs between Manitoba and the Northwest Angle consists of using a telephone to call either the Canadian or United States customs agency to make a border crossing declaration!

Superior National Forest was established in 1909.

The region also includes the Mesabi Range. These reddish, rocky hills zigzag 110 miles (180 km) from Babbitt in the northeast to Grand Rapids in the southwest. The range gets its name from an Ojibwa legend about a red giant named Mesabi who slept in the earth. In 1887, a miner discovered iron ore in the range. Minnesota soon became one of America's key iron-mining states. Some of the world's oldest rocks can be found here, remnants of lava that flowed from volcanoes

The Iron Range has a
distinctive appearance.

The source of the
Mississippi River is
located in Minnesota.

about 2.7 billion years ago. This lava formed
the foundation of the Iron Range in Northern
Minnesota. (The Iron Range includes the Mesabi
Range as well as three other major iron deposits.)

North-central Minnesota also has mixed
forests of evergreen and deciduous trees. In
addition, this area has many lakes and large areas
of wetlands. The source of the Mississippi River,
Lake Itasca, is located in this region. People come
long distances to Minnesota's oldest state park,
Itasca State Park, to walk across the mighty river
at its source. There, the river is just a trickle,
and visitors can step across from stone to stone.
From Lake Itasca, the Mississippi travels south
about 2,320 miles (3,730 km) to reach the Gulf
of Mexico. The Mississippi is the largest river
in North America in terms of volume of water
carried.

The Deciduous Forests

In the southeast and through a band extending
diagonally into the center of the state is a
region of deciduous forests that include maple,
ash, oak, and elm trees. The region has open
woods and scattered prairies. The Saint Croix,
Minnesota, and other large rivers have cut
deep valleys through the landscape. They give
Minnesota some of its most dramatic scenery.
The region also contains a large amount of **fertile**
agricultural land.

The southeastern corner of Minnesota has
steep, forest-covered hills cut by deep streams that
rush down to join the Mississippi River. Drier
hillsides are covered with waving grasses. The last
set of glaciers from the north missed this area of
Minnesota, leaving it much more rugged than the
rest of the state. The region is sometimes called
the Driftless area.

The Prairie Grassland

Western Minnesota is generally drier than eastern parts of the state. For this reason, prairie grasslands rather than forests are the main ecosystem. The prairie grasslands consist of grasses up to 8 feet (2.4 m) tall, such as big bluestem. About ten thousand years ago, the northern part of the prairie grassland area was at the bottom of part of a huge lake called Lake Agassiz. The lake formed as the glaciers melted. A few thousand years later, the lake drained. At that time, the deepest part of the lake became a flat, fertile plain. Today, the Red River flows across this region. The Red River valley is known for its oats, corn, and bright-yellow sunflowers. Farther south, the prairie grassland consists of a plateau of quartz bedrock.

The Saint Croix River flows through Minnesota and Wisconsin.

The Tallgrass Aspen Parkland

The aspen woods and prairies in part of northwestern Minnesota make up the smallest of the state's natural regions. This region forms a transition between the mixed forests to the east and the tallgrass prairies to the west. The area also was once covered by Lake Agassiz. However, the lake was shallower here than it was to the west. The lake bottom was made up mainly of sand or rocks. To this day, the soil is less fertile than southern and central Minnesota. Today, it's more common to find cattle grazing than crops growing.

Big bluestem prairie grass can grow to an astonishing height.

Minnesota's Varied Climate

Minnesotans joke that their state's climate has two seasons: winter and road construction. Snow

The Red River valley

Waterfalls and Wild Rice

French explorers were the first Europeans to reach the land that became Minnesota. One explorer, Father Louis Hennepin, wrote a book about his journey. *A New Discovery of a Vast Country in America, Volume 1* was published in 1697. In the book, Hennepin describes encountering "a fall of fifty or sixty foot [15–18 m], which we called the Fall of St. Anthony of Padua, whom we had taken for the protector of our discovery." (Hennepin exaggerates the waterfall's height.) Hennepin also describes encountering wild rice, which he calls "wild oats," farther north:

> The country about the Lake Issati is a marshy ground, wherein grows **abundance** of wild oats, which grow without any culture or sowing, in lakes, provided they are not above 3 foot [0.9 m] deep. That corn is somewhat like our oats but much better; and its stalks are a great deal longer when it is ripe.

This statue of Father Louis Hennepin is in Minneapolis.

Setting the Borders

The French claimed the territory of Minnesota in 1679. In 1763, the French **ceded** their possessions east of the Mississippi River to the British. In 1783, the British ceded this land to the United States in the Treaty of Paris, which formally ended the Revolutionary War. However, the land boundaries in the Treaty of Paris contained a mistake. The people who worked out the treaty used a map that showed the wrong shape for Lake of the Woods. That mistake later led to the creation of the area called the Northwest Angle!

In 1803, the United States bought the land to the west of the Mississippi River from France in the Louisiana Purchase. In 1818, the United States and Great Britain agreed that the land included in the Louisiana Purchase, which included the western half of present-day Minnesota, had a northern border with Canada at the 49th parallel (49° N).

The eastern half of Minnesota's northern border was defined in 1842 in the Webster-Ashburton Treaty. The treaty drew a border following a traditional trade route from Lake Superior to the northwestern point of Lake of the Woods. From this point, the border heads due south to the 49th parallel, the border of the western United States and Canada. The treaty added 123 square miles (318.6 sq km) to Minnesota on the northern side of Lake of the Woods, the Northwest Angle. The western half of Minnesota's northern border follows the 49th parallel to North Dakota.

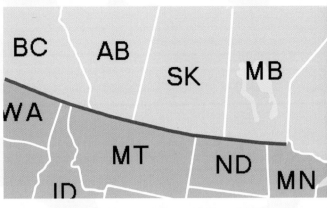

The red line on this map is the 49th parallel. Above the line are the Canadian provinces of British Columbia, Alberta, Saskatchewan, and Manitoba. Below are the US states of Washington, Idaho, Montana, North Dakota, and Minnesota.

The state's western border was set by Minnesota territorial delegate Henry M. Rice. He thought a state that had a long north–south border would create a state with a diverse economy based on different natural resources (lumber, agriculture, and mining).

The southern border was created when Iowa gained statehood in 1846. Iowa voters chose the boundary because it nestled Iowa between the Mississippi River to the east and the Missouri and Big Sioux Rivers to the west.

The eastern border with Wisconsin was set by moving south from the Saint Louis River, near the western tip of Lake Superior, to the Saint Croix River. The border follows the Saint Croix to the Mississippi River, at which point the Mississippi becomes the eastern border. Many Wisconsin residents wanted the border between the two states to follow the Mississippi River all the way north to Lake Itasca and up to Canada. Congress chose otherwise.

In 1947, Minnesota, Michigan, and Wisconsin defined boundaries within Lake Superior.

Minnesotans don't let winter weather stop them from staying active.

Skyways connect buildings so that commuters can avoid the cold.

covers much of the state from mid-December to mid-March. The snowiest part of Minnesota is along Lake Superior. That part of the state gets an average of about 7 feet (2.1 meters) of snow every winter. Even the drier southwestern region averages 3 feet (0.9 m) of snow each year. With Minnesota's cold winters, the snow sticks around. In Minneapolis, which is in the southeastern part of the state, January temperatures average 15.6 degrees Fahrenheit (–9.1 degrees Celsius). The average winter has 22.5 days when the temperature falls to 0°F (–18°C) or lower. Places in northern Minnesota from time to time report winter temperatures close to –40°F (–40°C).

In the downtown districts of Minnesota's larger cities, people use skyways. These enclosed, aboveground walkways between buildings help people avoid the cold. The rest of Minnesota doesn't have that luxury. The cold can be unpleasant. Yet for those who love winter sports, Minnesota is a paradise. Snow-covered hills are great for sledding and downhill skiing. Forest paths are used for cross-country skiing and snowmobiling. Frozen lakes provide places to skate and play hockey. When the ice gets thick enough, many Minnesotans walk out on the surface and go fishing. They cut holes in the ice to drop in fishing lines. When the ice gets really thick, ice fishers drive onto the lake and set up an ice-fishing shack.

Summer may come as a relief to many Minnesotans, but it is not always a reward. The average low in Minneapolis in July is 64°F (18°C). The average high temperature is 83°F (28°C). However, it can get much hotter than that. The temperature in Minneapolis has gone as high as 108°F (42°C). In Moorhead on July 6, 1936, the temperature reached a record high for the state, hitting 114°F (46°C). Given that the lowest recorded temperature recorded in Minnesota was –60°F (–51°C), Minnesota has one of the largest temperature ranges of any state.

Minnesotans who prefer cooler weather can head to the shores of Lake Superior during the summer. The surface of the massive lake acts like a giant air conditioner, cooling the air above it. The air then blows onshore and cools shore areas to comfortable levels. It is also common for Minnesotans to own a lake cabin (or know someone who does) at any of the thousands of lakes in the state.

Ice fishers make the most of cold winters.

Minnesota's Wildlife

Minnesota's different ecosystems allow for a wide variety of plants and animals. Bluestem grasses, blazingstar flowers, black-eyed Susans, and prairie smoke flowers are among the many colorful plants that brighten the prairie. Trees add year-round interest. Oaks and aspen trees are common in the deciduous and mixed forests. In summer, their leaves shimmer in the breeze. Maple trees grow in many parts of the state. In the fall, their leaves turn beautiful shades of orange, red, and yellow. Pine, spruce, and other evergreen trees dominate parts of northern and eastern Minnesota. In the winter, they add dark beauty to the snow-covered Minnesota landscape.

The fields and forests are also home to deer, beavers, raccoons, and squirrels. In the woods, you may see skunks, martens, porcupines, and red and gray foxes. The howls of wolves and coyotes often pierce the night. Larger animals include moose, elk, and black bears.

Minnesota has a large bird population. Common songbirds such as robins, cardinals, goldfinches, and many others nest in the state. Water-loving species, including Canada geese, mallards, and wood ducks, also abound. In addition, the state lies at the northern edge of

FAST FACT
Minnesota rivers and streams flow in three directions: north to Canada, south to the Gulf of Mexico, and east to the Atlantic Ocean. The East Savanna River, for example, flows from Wolf Lake east to the Saint Louis River, Great Lakes, and Atlantic. The Red River flows north along the North Dakota border to Lake Winnipeg.

Minnesota's Biggest Cities

(Population numbers are from the US Census Bureau's 2017 projections.)

1. Minneapolis: population 422,331

Minneapolis is the largest city in Minnesota. It is often called the "City of Lakes." The area includes twenty lakes and wetlands, creeks, and the Mississippi River. It is the primary business center between Chicago and Seattle.

2. Saint Paul: population 306,621

Saint Paul is the capital of Minnesota. It is located just east of Minneapolis. These two cities are known as the "Twin Cities." The Minneapolis–Saint Paul area is one of the top-twenty largest metropolitan areas in the United States.

3. Rochester: population 115,733

Rochester, southeast of Minneapolis, was named a "Best Small City" by *Money* magazine. It said, "One thing to remember about Rochester is that it has the sophistication of a larger metro area, but not the congestion or the complications."

4. Duluth: population 86,066

Duluth sits on the shore of Lake Superior, making it a popular place for people to visit. The city has theaters, concerts, and shopping. Duluth is frequently ranked as one of the best and most affordable places to live in America.

5. Bloomington: population 85,866

Located on the banks of the Minnesota River, Bloomington is home to the famous Mall of America. The city also has the Minnesota Valley National Wildlife Refuge, Water Park of America, and hiking and biking trails.

Minneapolis

Bloomington

6. Brooklyn Park: population 80,581

Located along the Mississippi River, Brooklyn Park features around 2,000 acres (809 ha) of parks, several golf courses, and 120 miles (193 km) of trails. Many people who work in the Minneapolis–Saint Paul area live in this quiet suburb.

7. Plymouth: population 78,395

A suburb of Minneapolis, Plymouth offers lakes, trails, good school districts, and quiet neighborhoods. The city has been ranked twice on *Money* magazine's list of "America's Best Places to Live."

8. Maple Grove: population 71,066

Maple Grove is a twenty-minute drive from Minneapolis, making it a popular and fast-growing suburb. Maple Grove boasts a popular farmers' market, numerous family-friendly events, and forty-eight playgrounds.

9. Woodbury: population 69,756

Woodbury, just outside Saint Paul, features 3,000 acres (1,214 ha) of parkland, forty community and neighborhood parks, and a swimming beach. The city is home to some major companies, including one of Dean Foods' biggest plants.

Saint Cloud

10. Saint Cloud: population 67,984

Saint Cloud calls itself the economic, social, and cultural heart of the state. It is a community with deep roots in agriculture and granite production. The area features the latest in health care, education, and technology.

Blazing star flowers are native to Minnesota.

The number of red-headed woodpeckers in Minnesota has dropped in recent years.

the Mississippi flyway, a long **migration** route taken by birds as they travel to and from their winter homes farther south. Over 250 species of birds migrate through Minnesota every year.

However, some birds that had been very common in Minnesota have begun to drop in numbers. For example, eastern meadowlarks, red-headed woodpeckers, and northern pintail ducks all are on the decline. Scientists think these birds have fewer good places to find food and to nest because more people now settle or vacation on grasslands, in woods, and along waterways. Minnesotans are working to keep wild lands wild. They also plant native species of flowers, trees, and shrubs in their yards and parks to help attract birds.

Aquatic, or water-loving, animals thrive in Minnesota. Several types of salamanders, frogs, snakes, and turtles live in and around the state's waterways. Minnesota's waters are home to many fish species, and the state has a big sports fishing industry. Minnesota sells more fishing licenses for the size of its population than any other state. Among the most popular fish are walleye, northern pike, bass, and muskie.

A Diverse Bounty

Minnesota's diverse geography and climate create adventure for those who live, visit, and vacation in the state. Even in the middle of the state's largest cities, Minneapolis and Saint Paul, the Mississippi River offers city dwellers daily contact with breathtaking natural beauty. The riverbanks are covered in forests and cliffs. The river tumbles down numerous waterfalls as it passes through the metropolitan area. Farther from cities, forests and prairies provide food, resources, and a quieter way of life.

Minnesota's Mall of America is a one-of-a-kind attraction. It is the largest shopping establishment in the United States. Inside, you can find almost anything you could ever want to buy. Specialty shops and boutiques are packed into the building. In all, there are more than five hundred places to go shopping. As a bonus, there is no sales tax on shoes or clothing, making it cheaper to splurge.

The Mall of America

Visitors can also find nearly any kind of entertainment they desire. There is an aquarium, an indoor amusement park, and FlyOver America—a virtual flight over the country. Also, there are more than sixty restaurants where you can get a bite to eat.

The Mall of America is quite easy to visit. It is very close to the Minneapolis–Saint Paul Airport, making it easy for people on long layovers to stop by and experience the shopping extravaganza. It is also a short train ride away from Minneapolis, so locals can visit again and again.

The Mall of America is one of Minnesota's biggest tourist attractions.

It's no surprise that the Mall of America is Minnesota's most popular tourist attraction. It draws in forty million visitors each year. Some come for the special events that the mall hosts. But most just come to see and shop at the sprawling complex of stores and entertainment.

What Lives in Minnesota?

Oak trees in
Big Woods State Park

Tamarack trees

Flora

Oak Trees   Oak trees are the most common hardwood trees in the Big Woods that extend from southeastern Minnesota up to the Canadian border. The most common types of oak tree in Minnesota are the northern red oak, northern pin oak, bur oak, and white oak.

Prairie Grasses   Tall prairie grasses native to Minnesota include Indian grass and big bluestem. Southwestern Minnesota was once covered by tallgrass prairieland. These grasses usually grow to between 4.9 feet and 6.6 feet (1.5 m and 2 m) tall. They can even reach as high as 8.2 feet to 9.8 feet (2.5 m to 3 m). This is several feet taller than an average human!

Red (Norway) Pine Trees   Red pine trees grow across northern and northeastern Minnesota. Mature trees stand 70 to 80 feet (21 to 24 m) tall. The species did not actually originate in Norway. Small red pines are popular Christmas trees. Mature trees are used for construction, such as structural beams or railroad ties. They can live to four hundred years old.

Tamarack Trees   Tamarack trees grow in Minnesota's northern swamps. The bark is thin and forms reddish brown scales. Minnesota has the largest recorded tamarack tree in the nation.

White Spruce Trees   The white spruce is commonly found in the northern forests and south to the Saint Croix Valley. It produces short bluish needles that turn bluish green as the tree matures. The trees typically grow to 40 feet to 50 feet (12 to 15 m) but can reach as tall as 100 feet (30 m).

Fauna

Bald Eagles   Minnesota has the largest bald eagle population of any state in the continental United States. In 2017, Minnesota had about 9,800 pairs of bald eagles who typically return to the same nest each year. Some stay in Minnesota year-round. Bald eagles build nests that are 6 to 8 feet (1.8 to 2.4 m) across. They usually lay one to three eggs in late winter.

Gray Wolves   Northeastern Minnesota was once home to the last remaining wild wolves in the continental United States. After wolves were declared an **endangered** species, the population of these wolves rebounded. They spread into northern Wisconsin and Michigan's Upper Peninsula. The wolf is fascinating and important to the ecosystem.

Gray wolf

Moose   Minnesota is one of the only states with moose. Moose are the largest wild animal in Minnesota and typically weigh around 1,000 pounds (453 kilograms). Moose primarily live in northern Minnesota along streams and lakes. Moose can run up to 35 miles per hour (56 kilometers per hour) and can swim for more than 10 miles (16 km) at a time.

Walleye   Walleye is the state fish of Minnesota. Minnesotans eat more walleye than people in any other state in the country. The walleye is typically brownish-yellow and between 15 inches and 24 inches (38 to 61 centimeters) long.

Moose

White-Tailed Deer   White-tailed deer are found in every county in Minnesota. Deer are commonly hunted for sport and food throughout the state. Adult males weigh between 100 and 300 pounds (45 to 136 kg). Females weigh between 85 and 130 pounds (39 to 59 kg). In the nineteenth century, deer were hunted so much they became rare in Minnesota. New rules allowed populations to grow again.

In this illustration, Paleoindians hunt a mastadon. Paleoindians were Minnesota's first residents.

2 The History of Minnesota

Archaeologists have divided the history of Minnesota into four cultural traditions. The earliest inhabitants of Minnesota were the Paleoindians. Paleoindians arrived in North America at least fourteen thousand years ago. They crossed over a land bridge that existed in the Bering Sea at the end of the last ice age. After arriving in Minnesota, they lived in the state from 9000 BCE to 5000 BCE. Paleoindians hunted large game using stone tools. According to the Minnesota Historical Society, the climate changed and populations of large animals dwindled over time. In the Archaic period that lasted from around 5000 BCE to 500 BCE, early Minnesotans began to hunt a diverse range of animals and fish. They also began to grow plants. Some Archaic peoples near the Great Lakes started to mine copper.

The next tradition was that of the Woodland people from 500 BCE to 1700 CE. The Woodland tradition began farther south and spread upward to Minnesota. The Woodland peoples began to farm crops including maize (an ancestor to corn). They also made items such as beads, copper figures, ceramic pottery, and the bow and arrow. The Woodland people buried their dead in burial mounds and began to build homes and settlements. In the seventeenth century, European explorers arrived. These explorers signaled a drastic change in the history and population of Minnesota.

The Native Minnesotans

Grand Mound is a sacred burial site.

Before the arrival of Europeans, many generations of Native Americans in the region (whose various tribes made up the Woodland people) gathered plants, fished, and hunted wild animals for food and clothing. They learned to carve stone and bone and later to shape copper into tools. To honor their dead, later groups started burying them in huge mounds made of earth. Some of these mounds are still visible today. One of the largest is Grand Mound, near International Falls. It is 140 feet (43 m) long, 100 feet (30 m) wide, and 25 feet (7.6 m) tall. It also has a 200-foot (61 m) tail that suggests the mound was shaped like an animal, perhaps a muskrat. Mounds with animal or other symbolic shapes are called effigy mounds.

Forests dominated the northern and eastern parts of Minnesota, and prairies were established in the west. Native peoples in the prairies developed a nomadic lifestyle centered on hunting deer and bison (sometimes called buffalo). Groups that spent more time near lakes developed a more settled lifestyle based on fishing.

Over time, these different lifestyles became more complex. Groups in north-central, northeastern, and east-central Minnesota began to harvest wild rice in addition to hunting and fishing. They found ways to store the rice by roasting it. This helped them to have more food in the winter months. Native Americans formed semipermanent settlements near the shallow bodies of water where wild rice grows. Groups that lived in the river valleys of southeastern Minnesota planted squash, beans, and corn in the fertile soil. These crops could also be prepared for winter storage.

Agriculture based on corn and beans became very important to Native Americans living in what is now southern Minnesota. They built large, permanent villages near their gardens. They also went on trips north to hunt, fish, and gather wild foods.

By the time the first Europeans arrived in North America, Native Americans in what is now Minnesota had been following the same cultural patterns for centuries. There were several major groups. The Iowa lived in the river valleys of the southeast. The Dakota lived in central Minnesota. The Ojibwa named these people Sioux—which means "little snakes" and implies "enemy." Today, however, many Dakota people associate the word with courage and use it proudly, such as the Shakopee Mdewakanton Sioux community in Minnesota. The Dakota were related to the Assiniboine, who lived in northwestern Minnesota. Another group, the Cheyenne, lived just north of the Dakota, between the Upper Mississippi River and Lake Mille Lacs.

The Europeans soon started trading with tribes. The Native Americans provided animal furs, which were very popular in Europe for coats and hats. Furs were exchanged for strong, durable tools, pots, and weapons made of iron. This trade was profitable for both groups. But it led to fierce competition among Native American tribes as well as among the European nations.

By 1660, tribes from the East such as the Ojibwa were pushing westward into the area. One of their main goals was to expand their fur-hunting grounds. They came into conflict with the tribes already living there. As the fur trade grew,

Native Americans settled where wild rice was growing. Wild rice continues to grow in Minnesota today.

The Dakota and the Ojibwa

The Dakota and Plains Ojibwa lived in the Great Plains in tepees made of bison hide, which made it easy to move from place to place. They followed the bison and depended on the bison for food, clothing, shelter, and many other resources. The Dakota were skilled artisans known for their quillwork, beadwork, pottery, and bison-hide paintings. The Dakota were also known for their impressive feathered war bonnets. Each feather was earned through an act of bravery and occasionally dyed red for a special accomplishment. The Dakota made their canoes out of dugout logs.

The woodland Ojibwa lived a more settled life farther north. Their homes were wigwams. Wooden frames were covered in birch bark to make these houses. The Ojibwa mined and traded copper, harvested wild rice, fished, and hunted wild game. They also harvested vegetables, such as squash and corn, and made sugar and maple syrup. They crafted canoes from birch bark. The Ojibwa additionally made beautiful floral beadwork, birch bark boxes, baskets, and dream catchers.

The Ojibwa were members of a powerful, longstanding alliance with two related tribes from the Great Lakes region of the US and Canada. The alliance was called the **Council** of Three Fires. The council was able to resist land takeover by both other Native groups and, to a large extent, Europeans. The Ojibwa were never relocated to Oklahoma and Kansas like many other tribes. Today, nearly all Ojibwa reservations are located within their original territory.

The Native Americans of Minnesota, like all other Native people in North America, were removed from their lands. The Dakota were almost entirely exiled from the state after the US-Dakota War in 1862. The Ojibwa were forced onto reservations. In the 1880s, Dakota people started moving back to Minnesota. The US government created four small Dakota reservations in addition to the state's seven Ojibwa reservations.

The eleven Native American tribes in Minnesota currently recognized by the US government include the Bois Forte Band of Chippewa, Fond Du Lac

Reservation, Grand Portage Band of Chippewa Indians, Leech Lake Band of Ojibwe, White Earth Reservation, Red Lake Band of Chippewa Indians, Lower Sioux Indian Community, Mille Lacs Band of Ojibwe, Prairie Island Indian Community, Shakopee Mdewakanton Sioux Community, and the Upper Sioux Community.

This photograph shows an Ojibwa family in 1913.

Spotlight on the Ojibwa

Historians think the name "Ojibwa" refers to either a type of moccasins the Ojibwa wore or their **custom** of writing on the bark of birch trees. The Ojibwa call themselves Anishinaabe, which means "first" or "original people." Oral tradition tells that the Ojibwa migrated from the mouth of the Saint Lawrence River west along the Great Lakes. A prophecy told them that lighter skinned people would come. The prophecy told them that to keep their traditions alive, the Anishinaabe must move west until they reached a land where food grows on water (which they found in Minnesota's wild rice).

Organization   Early Ojibwa communities were based on clans, which determined a member's place in the Ojibwa society. Different clans represented different parts of their society. Warriors were generally from the Bear clan. Scouts came from the Wolf clan. Political leaders came from the Loon or Crane clans.

Maple Syrup   The Ojibwa made maple sugar and syrup. Traditionally, women did the sugar-making. From February to April, sap ran freely in the sugar maple trees. Every day during this time, the women gathered sap and carried it to a special wigwam where it was processed. The Ojibwa then made either syrup, sugar, or maple sugar cakes.

Clothing   Ojibwa women wore long dresses. Ojibwa men wore breechcloths and leggings. Both men and women wore moccasins on their feet. In later years, the tribe wore clothing made from **imported** cloth they had traded with the Europeans.

Henry Sibley was governor of Minnesota during the final Dakota-Ojibwa battle. He ordered the Dakota back to their reservation to end the strife.

Lake Winnibigoshish is just one example of a place name that comes from the Ojibwa language.

more tribes became involved. Conflicts intensified. The Dakota became pressured by the Ojibwa, who came into the region from the area north and east of Lake Superior. The Ojibwa pushed the Dakota south and west as they moved into the state.

The Dakota and the Ojibwa had competed for resources for decades. They fought and made peace many times. Competition over the fur trade made them bitter enemies. As the Ojibwa settled onto Dakota lands, the Dakota were gradually forced out of the northern half of what is now Minnesota. The final Dakota-Ojibwa battle took place on May 27, 1858. The governor of Minnesota, Henry Sibley, commanded the Dakota back to their reservation to separate the tribes and prevent future fighting.

While the Native American population is a fraction of what it once was, many places in Minnesota show their former presence. The cities of Shakopee, Cokato, Chanhassen, and Chaska all get their names from Dakota words. Many place names start with "Minne," including Minnesota, the cities of Minnetonka and Minnetrista, and Minnehaha Falls. All are Dakota words that incorporate *mni*, which is a Dakota word meaning "water." (Minneapolis is a combination of *mni* and the Greek word *polis*, which means "city." This blend means "City of Water.") Other place names come from the Ojibwa, such as the word Mississippi. That name comes from the Ojibwa word *mishisibi*, which means "large river." Lake Winnibigoshish is also an Ojibwa place name, as is Kanabec County and the township of Ottawa.

The French Fur Trade

The French set up fur-trading posts in eastern Canada in the early 1600s and explored many parts of North America. The first Europeans to reach the area that is now Minnesota were the

French fur traders Pierre-Esprit Radisson and Médard Chouart des Groseilliers. Radisson and Groseilliers traveled from Montreal to the

This illustration shows Pierre-Esprit Radisson and Médard Chouart des Groseilliers meeting with Native Americans.

Great Lakes and back from 1654 to 1660. They were in search of the Northwest Passage—a water route linking the Atlantic and Pacific Oceans. There was no Northwest Passage through the Great Lakes. Instead, they found deep forests and abundant waterways. In 1659, they reached the western tip of Lake Superior at present-day Duluth.

In 1679, Daniel Greysolon, sieur Du Lhut (also spelled Duluth), began a long journey through the area. He believed that the French needed to trade with the tribes living west of the Great Lakes. He also wanted to establish peace among warring Native American tribes. Doing so, he believed, would benefit the French fur trade. Du Lhut made it to Duluth (named after him). There he spent months with Dakota and Ojibwa tribes. In 1680, Du Lhut traveled down the Saint Croix River to the Mississippi River. Once he arrived, he learned that the Dakota had captured the explorer Father Louis Hennepin and two other Frenchmen. Du Lhut bartered for the men's freedom. Du Lhut was then forced to return back to Quebec and then France. He faced accusations of treason, as he had been trading with tribes without government approval. Even so, Du Lhut's work helped strengthen French control over the area that is now Minnesota.

In the next century, French traders traveled throughout the region. They soon came into conflict with the British. Both nations competed to build a fur-trading empire in North America. By 1754, the competition between Britain and

France had erupted into the French and Indian War. This conflict, which also involved Native American tribes, ended in defeat for France in 1763. Under the treaty ending the war, Britain officially gained control of nearly all the land that France had claimed in North America east of the Mississippi River, including present-day eastern Minnesota. Eventually, most of the French moved from this area. Today, French place names are common in Minnesota, such as Marquette Avenue and Nicollet Island in Minneapolis, Hennepin County, and the towns of Saint Paul, Elysian, Cloquet, and Belle Plaine. The French names are a reminder of the country's significance in Minnesota's history.

George Washington leads a prayer during the French and Indian War.

From British Territory to American State

In 1775, the American colonists began their successful war for independence from Great Britain. The Revolutionary War officially ended with the Treaty of Paris in 1783. Under the peace treaty, the new United States gained control of lands east of the Mississippi River. This included present-day eastern Minnesota.

In 1803, the United States bought the Louisiana Territory from France. This action—known as the Louisiana Purchase—added a huge area west of the Mississippi River to the United States. The purchase included most of the rest of what became the state of Minnesota.

The Treaty of Paris, shown here, marked the end of the American Revolution.

In the early 1800s, the United States purchased an important piece of land from the Dakota along the Mississippi River. It included Saint Anthony Falls and the strategic spot where the Minnesota River flows into the Mississippi River. The river junction had long been a sacred gathering place for Native Americans.

Saint Anthony Falls

The United States Army arrived at the spot in 1819. Under the command of Colonel Josiah Snelling, they built a fort there. The sturdy outpost was named Fort Saint Anthony after the nearby waterfalls. After Snelling's death, the fort was renamed in his honor.

After Fort Snelling was built, European American settlers began arriving. The region around the fort had the state's earliest European American post office, school, and hospital. It also had a flour mill and a lumber mill. In time, the settlements in the area became the cities of Minneapolis and Saint Paul. Because the water from Saint Anthony Falls drops 50 feet (15 m), there was a lot of energy for the mills to harness. The falls are the reason that Saint Paul and Minneapolis grew.

This growth was slow at first. The region was remote. It was very cold and isolated in winter. During the worst of winter, mail service and outside trade were spotty. But the area had many resources, including forests rich with timber. Much of the land was Native American territory. However, the US government continued to

Fort Snelling is now a National Historic Landmark.

pressure the Native American nations to give up land. The Iowa ceded all of their Minnesota land to the government between 1820 and 1840. Treaties signed by the Ojibwa in 1851 required most of them to leave their forests in the upper half of the region. The Dakota sold all their land east of the Red River. In return, they received only a small strip of land along the Minnesota River.

With the Native Americans relocated, more settlers wanted to move to the region. Steamboat travel to the area increased, and many boats landed at a dock near Fort Snelling known as Pig's Eye Landing. In 1841, a Roman Catholic **missionary** built a small church nearby and dedicated it to Saint Paul. The area developed into a booming port settlement and was named Saint Paul, after the mission church. Saint Paul became the capital of the Minnesota Territory in 1849.

From 1850 to 1854, the population grew very slowly. Many **immigrants** headed to California to seek gold. Between 1853 and 1857, however, the region's European American population grew from 40,000 to 150,000 people. Part of this success was due to Minnesota's first commissioner of emigration, Eugene Burnand. Burnand met new immigrants in New York City and encouraged them to move to Minnesota. In 1858, Minnesota became the thirty-second state. Saint Paul was chosen as the capital.

Wars Near and Far

The new state continued to grow into the 1860s, though at a slower pace than in the 1850s. Small farms sprouted on the plains. Villages sprang up along waterways. The telegraph connected distant towns. The US government offered railroad companies millions of acres of land to build a network of railroads across the West. The railroad companies also needed cash, however. They looked for people willing to purchase the land they had been granted. The railroad companies arranged to have steamship lines bring European, mostly Scandinavian, immigrants into Minnesota. The immigrants provided the cash the railroads needed to get to work. After establishing farms and businesses, they also became customers.

Abraham Lincoln's Homestead Act brought many immigrants to Minnesota.

In 1862, Abraham Lincoln signed a law called the Homestead Act. It granted 160 acres (65 ha) of land in the American Midwest or Far West to anyone who agreed to build and live on the land for five years. Many immigrants came to Minnesota from western and northern Europe, especially Sweden, Norway, and Germany. They were eager to own land and start farms in the new state.

From 1861 to 1865, the American Civil War raged between the Northern (Union) and Southern (Confederate) states. As one of the newest states, Minnesota had just 180,000 citizens. Nonetheless, Minnesota sent 24,000 soldiers to fight for the Union. Those soldiers included free black men and Native Americans. The Union's victory in 1865 resulted in the end of slavery in the United States. It also kept the nation whole.

Meanwhile, a different battle raged on Minnesota soil between the Dakota and the settlers. The US government rarely kept its treaty promises. The Dakota received little in return for lands they had sold. As their lands shrank and food grew scarce, they grew hungrier and angrier. Then, on August 17, 1862, a small band of Dakota

A monument to Minnesota's Union soldiers stands in Gettysburg National Military Park in Pennsylvania.

Thaóyate Dúta was
a Dakota chief.

attacked settlers near Acton. Three white men and two white women died.

The Mdewakanton Dakota chief Thaóyate Dúta, known as Little Crow, approved a plan to push out white settlers. Thaóyate Dúta had originally supported peace. However, the US government had turned back on its promises time after time. Other Dakota believed this was a good time to chase out the settlers, since so many men were off fighting in the Civil War. Thaóyate Dúta knew the Dakota could not win. Yet he reluctantly agreed. Dakota warriors attacked farms and forts, burned buildings, and had a period of early success. On September 6, 1862, President Lincoln created the Department of the Northwest with orders to end the violence in Minnesota. One group of US forces was led by former governor Henry Sibley. Sibley spoke Dakota, hunted with Dakota men, and had a Dakota daughter. Now he fought against them.

Sibley's forces defeated Thaóyate Dúta and a force of Dakota in a final large-scale battle on September 23. Thaóyate Dúta and his soldiers fled the next day. By the time the Native Americans surrendered on September 26, they had taken 269 Americans captive. Between 450 and 800 settlers and 70 American soldiers had been killed. Approximately 75 to 100 Dakota warriors died fighting in the war. After they surrendered, 498 Dakota warriors were put on trial. Three hundred and three were sentenced to death. The Dakota had no attorneys. Some trials lasted less than five minutes. President Abraham Lincoln personally reviewed and reduced most of the sentences to prison terms. Lincoln upheld the **execution** of thirty-eight Dakota people. This was the biggest mass execution in US history. The army also rounded up 1,700 Dakota who had not been sentenced to death or prison. These included women, children, and elders, as well as warriors.

The army brought them to Fort Snelling, where they were kept for the winter. Almost 300 of the interned Dakota died that winter.

In the spring of 1863, the Dakota were sent from the state of Minnesota by the Dakota Expulsion Act. They went to lands with poor soils and few resources. The state also placed cash bounties on the Dakota. Thaóyate Dúta, who had returned to Minnesota, was killed by a bounty hunter near Hutchinson on July 3, 1863.

Farmers, Loggers, and Miners

In the mid-1860s, Minnesota started a period of rapid development. Land was cleared for farming in much of the southern, central, and western regions of the state. The settlers suffered many hardships, including **plagues** of grasshoppers from 1873 to 1877 that destroyed crops year after year. However, they worked hard to build a new life for themselves in this new land. By 1878, wheat, Minnesota's most important crop, accounted for nearly 70 percent of the state's farmland. This was good for the flour milling industry in Minneapolis. In fact, the city had become known as the flour milling capital of the world.

The logging industry started in central Minnesota in the mid-1800s. At first, Native Americans were the region's main lumberjacks. They cut down trees and sent them downriver to lumber mills. As loggers cleared more land, they moved farther north. The logging industry in Minnesota reached its peak around 1900, producing 2.3 billion feet (701 million meters) of lumber. Owners of lumber companies became rich. But they had cut down most of the state's white pines. One-third of Minnesota's total forests were gone.

This cartoon shows farmers fighting a plague of grasshoppers that threatened crops.

The "Iron Man" statue is in Chisholm.

In the late 1880s, a miner working for the Merritt family discovered a big deposit of iron in the Mesabi Range. Unlike other finds, this rich ore lay near the surface. It was easy to reach. The first mine soon opened. In time, Minnesota was supplying almost three-fourths of the nation's iron ore. Steelmaking also became an important industry in the state. In 1907, US Steel—one of the largest steel companies at the time—built a steel mill near Duluth. It opened in 1916 and was in operation for seventy-five years.

Workers Unite

Big companies began to dominate many Minnesota industries. These included mining, food processing, and manufacturing industries, as well as railroads. Factory workers often were paid low wages. They struggled to make a decent living. The first major call for change came from farmers. Farmers had to risk bad weather and make it through years of low prices for their crops. Additionally, farmers had to pay high rates to store their crops in giant towers called grain elevators. They paid heavily to ship their crops to market by rail too. They needed a way to reduce costs.

In 1867, a Minnesota farmer named Oliver H. Kelley began a group called the National Grange of the Order of Patrons of Husbandry. The group was designed to fight for the rights of the farmers. The Grange spread rapidly throughout Minnesota and other farm states. In two years, Minnesota had forty Grange chapters. By 1873, the Grange had nearly seven hundred thousand members across the country. Grange members bought equipment and supplies as a group. This lowered their costs. They pooled savings in an early form of a credit union.

Paul Bunyan was born in the tall tales of American loggers who told stories to fill the long days. The tales say that Paul Bunyan was a giant lumberjack who worked with his giant blue ox named Babe. Babe was blue from winter cold when Bunyan found him and brought him home. He stayed blue forever after. It was said Bunyan and Babe created Minnesota's lakes with their footsteps, which filled with rainwater. In some stories, Babe was pulling an enormous tank wagon when it began to leak. This created Lake Itasca and spilled over all the way to New Orleans, creating the Mississippi River. Tall tales also credit Bunyan and Babe with the creation of Puget Sound, the Grand Canyon, and the Black Hills.

The loggers said that Bunyan could cut entire acres of lumber in minutes by tying his axe to a rope and swinging it in circles. He had an enormous appetite, with a camp stove that covered an entire acre. Bunyan's hotcake griddle was so big it had to be greased using men with sides of bacon strapped to their feet like skates.

Today, Bemidji claims to be the birthplace of the mythical Paul Bunyan. Bemidji has an 18-foot (5.5 m) statue of Bunyan standing next to Babe the Blue Ox. Brainerd has Paul Bunyan Land, an amusement park with a talking Bunyan statue. Akeley, Minnesota, also claims to be the birthplace of Paul Bunyan. Akeley holds a Paul Bunyan Days festival each year to celebrate National Paul Bunyan Day. The idea for Paul Bunyan Days was born in 1955 when Rose Brewer Blood and Art Blood thought of it as a way to attract tourists to Akeley. The festival includes a fish fry, street dancing, a cakewalk, a pie social, and turtle racing. June 2018 was the seventieth anniversary of the festival.

National Paul Bunyan Day is commemorated across the United States on June 28.

National Paul Bunyan Day

Bemidji's Paul Bunyan

This 1873 print advertises the Grange.

Grange members lobbied and elected people to government offices who would pass laws to help farmers. These laws, called the Granger Laws, limited the rates railroad and grain elevator owners could charge farmers. The Grange helped farmers throughout the country gain political and economic power. Notably, the National Grange was the first national organization to require that women were represented in leadership. Thanks to Kelley's niece Caroline Hall, the national organization required that at least four of its sixteen elected positions be held by women.

Iron miners, predominantly immigrants from Finland, Austria-Hungary, and other European countries, also banded together. They wanted better working conditions and pay. Two famous strikes occurred on the Mesabi Range in 1907 and 1916. Walkouts also occurred among loggers and sawmill workers. Companies often responded by hiring new men called strikebreakers to work during the strike. This forced the striking workers to either give up their protests or lose their jobs.

Minnesota's most famous strike came when Minneapolis truckers walked off the job, calling for companies to recognize the General Drivers Local 574 chapter of the International Brotherhood of Teamsters union. The union had three thousand members. However, Minneapolis employers refused to recognize it or negotiate pay and working conditions. On July 20, 1934, police fired into a group of unarmed strikers. Two strikers died, and sixty-seven were wounded. The day became known as Bloody Friday. The event helped build support for labor unions in Minnesota and in the rest of the United States. In August, a settlement was reached that gave the union most of what it asked for.

Busts and Booms

By the 1930s, the Great Depression was in full swing. Life was hard for workers throughout the country. In Minnesota, large numbers of factory workers and miners lost their jobs. Farmers were also affected by the hard times. Crop prices fell more than 60 percent in the early 1930s. Rural Minnesotans were suffering. Some farmers could not afford to plant new crops. Many were at risk of losing their farms and homes. Some did. In September 1932, an organization of Minnesota farmers called the Farmers' Holiday Association (FHA) called a strike to get higher prices for their crops. They blockaded major roads to prevent food from being delivered to Minneapolis and Saint Paul. The next year, twenty thousand Minnesota farmers joined the FHA in marching on the state capitol in Saint Paul. This time, they helped get a law passed to block banks from taking farms away from families who owed money and could not repay their loans.

World War II (in which the United States fought from 1941 to 1945) helped end the Great Depression in Minnesota and the rest of the nation. The soldiers and the people of Great Britain needed food. As a result, agricultural prices rose significantly in the early 1940s. The military

FAST FACT

Charles Pillsbury started a flour mill in Minnesota in 1869. He launched one of the nation's first profit-sharing models when he shared Pillsbury profits with employees. He paid sometimes as much as $25,000 per year in bonuses (significant money in the 1800s). In 1889, the *New York Times* reported that "the men take a deeper interest in their work and seem content and happy." Pillsbury never had a workers' strike.

The Mahoning Mine in Hibbing was featured on a 1940s postcard.

needed equipment, and the demand for iron drove the Minnesota iron ranges to new production heights. Minnesota supplied 75 percent (or more) of the iron used for the war. For the first time, women were allowed to mine iron ore to meet production demands as men were drafted to fight. Another milestone came in 1959, when the Saint Lawrence Seaway opened. It allowed big ships from the Atlantic Ocean to sail all the way to Duluth at the western end of the Great Lakes. The seaway gave Minnesota's mines and other industries an international port.

Minnesota Tough

Minnesotans have a strong tradition of thinking independently and speaking out to express their views. Minnesota's own political party, the Farmer-Labor Party, was the most powerful party in the state during the early 1900s. It merged with the Democratic Party in 1944. The resulting Democratic-Farmer-Labor Party (DFL) continues to produce influential political leaders, especially in the US Senate. Minnesotans also showed their independence in 1998 when they elected

The first bridge ever built over the Mississippi River was a suspension bridge in Minnesota. It opened in 1855 where the Hennepin Avenue Bridge stands today. The modern bridge is a beautiful steel suspension bridge with blue design work.

Suspension bridges have two main cables. One cable is on each side of the bridge. They anchor into the ground and rise up between the bridge's towers. Suspender cables attach the bridge's deck (where the road or path is) to the main cables to hold the deck up.

The suspension bridge you'll build has just one set of towers and a main cable to illustrate how a suspension bridge works.

Make a Suspension Bridge

Materials:

- 6 straws
- Tape
- String
- 2 paper clips
- 2 chairs
- A ruler
- Scissors

Directions:

1. Cut two pieces of straw 1.25 inches (3 cm) long.
2. Take one short straw and two full straws and stand them up in a bundle. The short straw should be in the center. (All three straw pieces should be even at the base.)
3. Tape the bundle around the bottom and around the top to create a tall, narrow pyramid.
4. Repeat steps 2 and 3. These are your bridge towers.
5. Tape each tower to the edge of a chair.
6. Place the chairs about 7 inches (18 cm) apart.
7. Tie the center of a 4-foot (1.2 m) string around the middle of another straw.
8. Place this straw between the towers so that it rests on the short straws.
9. Take the string and drape each end over one tower and down to the surface of the chairs.
10. Wrap each end of the string around a paper clip and pull the paper clips away from the tower until the cable is pulled tightly.
11. Tape the paper clips to the surface of the chairs.
12. Use string and objects of your choice to see how much weight the deck of your bridge can hold!

Jesse "The Body" Ventura governor of Minnesota. Ventura was best known as a professional wrestler, sports commentator, and actor. In Minnesota, his legacy includes the construction of the state's first light rail line (a fast urban passenger train).

Jesse Ventura served as governor from 1999 to 2003.

Along with the rest of the nation, Minnesota suffered from a recession, or downturn in the economy. The recession began at the end of 2007 and then became more severe. The state lost 160,000 jobs. However, the unemployment rate, or percentage of workers who were out of work and looking for a job, was still lower than the average for the United States as a whole. After the recession ended, Minnesota added jobs much faster than the rest of the nation.

In the summer of 2016, Minnesota faced a heartbreaking tragedy that the whole nation watched. An African American man named Philando Castile was killed by a police officer during a traffic stop. The police officer, Jeronimo Yanez, said that the shooting was in self-defense. A video of the event raised questions, though. Yanez went to trial for the shooting and was acquitted (found not guilty). Protests took place in Minnesota and around the United States. Many Minnesotans came together, however, to work toward preventing such a tragedy from happening again.

Overall, the history of Minnesota contains tragedy, grit, and success. The Dakota, Iowa, Cheyenne, and Ojibwa were erased from their lands. The European immigrants and American settlers that moved in banded together to survive the Great Depression with their homes and livelihoods intact.

Today, the face of Minnesota is changing again. The immigrants arriving today are Latino, Somali, and Hmong. Many of these immigrants live in the Minneapolis–Saint Paul metropolitan area, but farther-flung areas are diversifying too. The next chapter of Minnesota's history is sure to be brighter thanks to this diversity.

FAST FACT
English theatrical director Sir Tyrone Guthrie opened the Guthrie Theater in Minneapolis in 1963. He wanted to create a theater that could be more innovative, experimental, and literary than a Broadway theater.

Important Minnesotans

James Ford Bell

James Ford Bell grew up in Minneapolis and studied chemistry at the University of Minnesota. He founded General Mills in 1928. Bell also served as chairman of the Milling Division of the Food and Drug Administration during World War I. As part of this work, he accompanied future president Herbert Hoover on a European Hunger Relief Mission trip in 1918.

James Ford Bell

F. Scott Fitzgerald

Fitzgerald was a writer born in Saint Paul in 1896. He is known for writing *The Great Gatsby* along with numerous other novels and short stories depicting the Jazz Age (the 1920s). Fitzgerald and his wife, Zelda Fitzgerald, famously lived large, dramatic lives in New York and on the French Riviera.

Judy Garland

Judy Garland is best known for playing Dorothy in *The Wizard of Oz*. She was born in Grand Rapids in 1922. Her original name was Frances Ethel Gumm. In fact, she began performing as part of the Gumm Sisters along with her two siblings. Garland was seventeen when she starred in *The Wizard of Oz*.

Judy Garland

Hubert H. Humphrey

Hubert H. Humphrey moved to Minneapolis from South Dakota to attend the University of Minnesota. He helped unite the state's Democratic and Farmer-Labor Parties. He became mayor of Minneapolis in 1945 and a United States senator in 1948. He was a senator for sixteen years, and was instrumental in passing the Nuclear Test Ban Treaty of 1963 and the Civil Rights Act of 1964. He served as vice president to Lyndon Johnson between 1965 and 1969.

Maud Hart Lovelace

Maud Hart Lovelace was born in Mankato in 1892. She began writing as a young child and sold her first short story at eighteen. She is known for her semiautobiographical *Betsy-Tacy* series of thirteen books. The *Betsy-Tacy* series is set in a fictional version of Mankato.

Charles Alfred Pillsbury

Pillsbury was born in New Hampshire before moving to Minnesota in 1869, where he founded a flour business. He improved the flour milling process and launched a brand called "Pillsbury's Best." Pillsbury helped make Minneapolis into one of the largest global markets for grain. He served in the Minnesota state senate.

Maud Hart Lovelace

Thaóyate Dúta, known as Little Crow

Thaóyate Dúta was a Dakota chief born in about 1810 in the Mdewakanton village of Kaposia. Thaóyate Dúta represented the Dakota in Washington, negotiating various treaties with the US government. He partially adopted European customs, including wearing some European clothing and living in a wooden house. He led the Dakota in a war against the US government.

Laura Ingalls Wilder

Laura Ingalls Wilder is the author of the beloved children's *Little House* series based on her childhood. Wilder was born in Wisconsin in 1867 and moved to Walnut Grove, Minnesota, with her family as a young girl. They lived there from 1874 to 1876 and again in 1878 and 1879 before moving to South Dakota.

Minnesota is proud of its diversity. Here, two Hmong girls enjoy Saint Paul.

3 Who Lives in Minnesota?

Minnesotans are famous for being nice, and data suggests the description is true. The Twin Cities are ranked first in the nation for volunteers. The entire state ranks second. Minnesota also ranks first for art funding per person, which may account in part for the number of successful musicians and writers who call Minnesota home. The state also stands at the top of national rankings for health care, population health, education, literacy, and more.

By the Numbers

Minnesota had more than 5.5 million people in 2017, making it the twenty-second most populated state. The population has shifted in recent decades from country to city living. Almost three-fourths of Minnesotans now live in an urban area.

Around 60 percent of the population lives in the Minneapolis–Saint Paul metropolitan area, which includes the Twin Cities and the many smaller cities and suburbs surrounding them. The area beyond the Twin Cities metropolitan area is often called Greater Minnesota.

FAST FACT

Prince made a movie called *Purple Rain*, which was filmed at First Avenue in Minneapolis. The movie opened July 27, 1984. The next month, Prince became the first artist to have a movie, album, and single ranked number one at the same time.

Raising the Bar

In Minnesota, people often bake a pan of bars to have around the house for dessert or to bring to an event. What are bars? They're much like cookies, but the dough is baked in a pan and sliced into squares or rectangles. Examples of popular bars in Minnesota include lemon bars, rhubarb bars, scotcheroos, and chocolate chip bars. Here's a classic chocolate chip bar recipe.

Ingredients:

- ½ cup butter, softened
- ½ cup brown sugar, packed
- ½ cup white sugar
- 1 egg (large)
- 2 teaspoons vanilla
- 1 cup flour
- ½ teaspoon baking soda
- ¼ teaspoon salt
- 1 cup semisweet chocolate chips

Instructions:

1. Preheat oven to 350°F.
2. In a large bowl (or using a stand mixer), beat the butter, brown sugar, and white sugar for four minutes or until mixture is fluffy.
3. Stir in egg and vanilla and mix well.
4. Stir in flour, baking soda, and salt. Stir just until flour is mixed in.
5. Stir in chocolate chips.
6. Bake for 28 to 34 minutes, or until golden brown.
7. Let cool for 10 minutes before cutting into squares.

Evolving Heritage

The face of Minnesota has changed over the years. The earliest residents were Native Americans. French Canadian fur trappers and missionaries were the first Europeans to arrive. In the 1800s, large numbers of German, Swedish, Norwegian, Danish, and Irish people settled in different parts of the state. The late 1800s also saw new waves of immigrants from eastern Europe, including Polish, Czech, and Finnish immigrants.

The Twin Cities are home to people from many different cultural backgrounds.

At first, members of these different ethnic groups spoke their own languages and kept to their old customs. When World War I broke out, for example, people living in New Ulm still spoke German in the country school and town stores. Many Minnesota Finns still have saunas in their home, and Swedes and Norwegians enjoy lutefisk dinners in Lutheran church basements. (Lutefisk, a fish preserved in lye, is now eaten more frequently in the United States than in its countries of origin.) These groups still preserve elements of their cultural heritage. But over the years, they begin blending in with the midwestern lifestyle.

Today, most Minnesotans are of European background. But there are also African Americans and Latinos. Many recent immigrants to Minnesota are from parts of Asia and Africa. These people make the state continually more culturally diverse.

Many immigrants came from Southeast Asia after the end of the Vietnam War in 1975. People from groups that had aided the American side during the war feared that they were in danger from Communist governments that had gained control of the region. Most of these immigrants were Hmong people from the mountains of Thailand, Vietnam, and Laos. Minnesota today

FAST FACT

Many people think of the movie *Fargo* when they think of Minnesota. Fargo is actually a city in North Dakota, but the movie does largely take place in Minnesota. Minnesota locations include Brainerd, Moose Lake, and Minneapolis. The film was originally named *Brainerd*.

Minnesota's Biggest Colleges and Universities

(All enrollment numbers are from US News and World Report 2018 college rankings.)

1. University of Minnesota Twin Cities, Minneapolis and Saint Paul
(34,871 undergraduate students)

2. Saint Cloud State University
(13,236 undergraduate students)

3. Minnesota State University, Mankato
(13,192 undergraduate students)

4. University of Minnesota Duluth
(9,967 undergraduate students)

5. Winona State University
(7,656 undergraduate students)

6. Southwest Minnesota State University, Marshall
(6,810 undergraduate students)

7. University of Saint Thomas, Saint Paul
(6,111 undergraduate students)

8. Minnesota State University Moorhead
(5,205 undergraduate students)

9. Bemidji State University
(4,795 undergraduate students)

10. University of Northwestern, Saint Paul
(3,241 undergraduate students)

University of Minnesota-Twin Cities

Winona State University

Bemidji State University

has more Hmong people than any other state except California. Saint Paul has the largest urban Hmong population in the country. In 2002, Mee Moua was elected to the Minnesota state senate, becoming the first-ever Hmong American state legislator.

Minnesota also has the largest Tibetan community in the United States outside New York. The state has also attracted many immigrants from African countries. The biggest group is from Somalia. War and poverty there have forced tens of thousands to leave their homeland. Today, tens of thousands of Somalis live in Minnesota, the largest population outside of East Africa. Minnesota also has one of the largest Ethiopian populations in the country. The Ethiopian population in Minnesota is one of the most diverse. (Like the United States, Ethiopia has many ethnic and religious groups. Many came to the United States as refugees of war and famine.)

Somali Americans pray before a Saint Paul soccer match in 2011.

One of the fastest growing immigrant groups in the state, however, is the Karen people. The Karen are an ethnic group that historically lived in Myanmar. Hundreds of thousands of Karen have fled Myanmar over recent decades after suffering killings, landmines, forced labor, and more at the hands of Myanmar's government. Church groups and others in Minnesota have helped immigrants resettle. The state has developed programs to meet the unique needs of immigrants and of **minorities**.

Adding to Minnesota's ethnic diversity are the more than seventy thousand Ojibwa, Dakota, and other Native Americans. Many live in the Twin Cities. Others live on reservations and elsewhere throughout the state.

An Ojibwa woman dances at a powwow in Inger, Minnesota.

Students at Lakeville South High School use technology as part of a science lesson.

Education

Surveys have ranked Minnesota near the top among US states in providing high-quality public schools. The state also ranks near the top for the percentage of residents who have graduated from high school.

Minnesota school officials and teachers have often been leaders in finding new ways to improve education. For example, in 1992, Minnesota became the first state to open a charter school. Charter schools are free public schools that are run separately from the traditional public school system. They try new or different teaching methods and were created to help more students do well in school.

In addition, public schools often have special programs devoted to the culture of particular ethnic groups. Many schools, especially in urban areas, provide classes in Spanish or certain African, Asian, or Native American languages to help meet the needs of students. High-performing high school students are also able to take some or all of their classes for free at local colleges or universities. This gives Minnesota students a chance to get part of a college degree at no cost to the student or family. It's also a great opportunity for high school students to take challenging classes.

FAST FACT

Imagine ninety-seven football fields. At 5.6 million square feet (520,000 square meters), the Mall of America in Bloomington is even bigger! The Mall of America draws more than forty million visitors each year.

Growth and Change

Minnesota has historically been home to Norwegians and Swedes. But today you're more likely to eat spring rolls or injera in Minneapolis than lefse (a Norwegian flatbread) or lutefisk. The population is constantly shifting as new groups of immigrants and refugees are attracted to the state's welcoming environment and strong economy.

In the 1860 census, Minnesota's population was overwhelmingly white and rural. Of the 172,000 state residents, 98 percent were white. Of these 172,000 people, just 16,000 lived in "cities" of 2,500 people or more.

Diversity in Minnesota

At first, the immigrants who came to Minnesota were mainly German, Norwegian, and Swedish. The Scandinavian immigration peaked around 1910, however. Today, the immigration patterns to Minnesota look vastly different. This change is making an impact on the state's make-up.

From 1990 to 2010, the number of Asian, black, and Hispanic residents in Minnesota grew four times larger. The fastest growing immigrant populations are people from Mexico, followed by the Hmong and people from India, Somalia, and Vietnam.

In 2006, Keith Ellison became the first Muslim elected to Congress.

In 2016 census estimates, about 20 percent of Minnesotans identified as people of color. In the Twin Cities, that number is 23 percent. It's the lowest diversity ranking of the nation's twenty-five largest metropolitan areas. However, it's predicted to change fast. By 2040, it's expected that 40 percent of the metropolitan area will be people of color.

Minnesota was the first state to elect a Muslim congressman. Keith Ellison was elected as a US representative in 2006. He continued to serve Minnesota's Fifth Congressional District until 2018, when he announced his plan to run for the position of state attorney general. When Ellison took his oath of office to enter Congress, he placed his hand on a Quran instead of a Bible. The Quran was once owned by Thomas Jefferson. (Jefferson was an advocate for religious freedom.)

The Celebrities of Minnesota

Ann Bancroft

Ann Bancroft is an American explorer from Saint Paul. She became the first woman to reach the North and South Poles on foot. Bancroft was born in Mendota Heights in 1955. In 1995, she joined the National Women's Hall of Fame. Today, she works with charitable organizations to help young women realize their full potential and to help all young people appreciate nature. The Ann Bancroft Foundation is one way she achieves these goals.

Ethan and Joel Coen

Joel and Ethan Coen

The Coen brothers are filmmakers well known for movies including *Fargo*, *The Big Lebowski*, and *No Country for Old Men*. They were born in Saint Louis Park. Joel is three years older than Ethan. The brothers are known for writing, directing, and producing their films. They have won Oscars for their writing and directing. In 2008, *No Country for Old Men* won the Best Picture award.

Doomtree

Doomtree is an independent hip-hop collective based in Minneapolis. The collective includes five rappers and two emcees. They also have their own record label.

Bob Dylan

Bob Dylan is a Nobel Prize–winning songwriter, singer, and artist. Dylan grew up as Robert Zimmerman in the northern Minnesota town of Hibbing. Dylan started his music career as a student at the University of Minnesota. His songs are often associated with protest movements.

Louise Erdrich

Louise Erdrich is a novelist and poet born in Little Falls. Many of her books explore her Chippewa heritage and ancestral history. She also owns a Minneapolis bookstore called Birchbark Books. In 2012, Erdrich won the National Book Award.

Josh Hartnett

Josh Hartnett is famous for starring in movies such as *Pearl Harbor* and *Black Hawk Down*. He was born and raised in Saint Paul. In addition to starring in movies, Hartnett has found success on the small screen. He appeared in *Penny Dreadful* as a main character for the duration of the series.

Prince

The music superstar Prince was born Prince Rogers Nelson in Minneapolis in 1958. Prince's hits include "Purple Rain" and "1999." Prince died in 2016. His death inspired tributes from around the globe.

Prince

Alec Soth

Alec Soth is an award-winning photographer born and based in Minneapolis. Some of his most famous portraits come from road trips along the Mississippi River from Minneapolis to New Orleans.

A researcher conducts an experiment at the Mayo Clinic in Rochester.

4 At Work in Minnesota

Minnesota is known for its impressive range of industries. The state has vibrant health care, education, agriculture, and mining industries, among others. This range of industries helps the state's economy weather hard times. Minnesota's economy doesn't depend on just one type of service or good.

Prominent Minnesota-based companies include Target, 3M (maker of the Post-it Note), General Mills, and Best Buy. The Mayo Clinic has a reputation around the world for treating the most difficult diseases. It is the state's largest employer. The state also draws in more than seventy million visitors each year who come to shop at the Mall of America, attend a Vikings or Twins game, canoe through the Boundary Waters, or relax at a cabin up north.

Farm Roots

Minnesota is a major farm state. The state's most valuable crops are field corn and soybeans. (Field corn is grown to feed livestock and make ethanol.) Minnesota is also a leading producer of wheat, oats, dried beans, flaxseeds, and sunflower

FAST FACT
The Post-it note was invented by Spencer Silver at 3M near Saint Paul. Silver was supposed to invent a tough new adhesive. He accidentally developed a sticky but removable adhesive instead. Years later, he used it to create a sticky bookmark for a colleague. They soon started using the bookmarks to write office notes. A product was born.

Minnesota farms are important to the state's economy.

seeds, among others. Year after year, it is the number-one grower of sugar beets, as well as sweet corn and peas for freezing or canning. Minnesota raises more turkeys than any other state. It is also a leading dairy and pork state.

Minnesota competes with California to be the nation's largest producer of cultivated wild rice. California, however, has no native beds of wild rice. In Minnesota, wild rice (which is actually a grass) naturally thrives in numerous lakes and marshes in large areas of the state. True wild rice is about three times more expensive at the grocery store than cultivated wild rice. This is partly because of the labor-intensive harvest process. The Ojibwa gather wild rice by paddling canoes through beds of wild rice and knocking the grains into the boat with sticks. They have used this technique for hundreds of years.

Native Americans gather wild rice in Leech Lake.

Farmers in Minnesota have had a long tradition of working together to grow and sell what they produce. To do this, they form organizations called cooperatives. Co-ops are organizations owned and operated by organization members. The farm cooperatives help farmers control costs better by buying resources in bulk or co-owning the resource production outright. The idea of cooperatives can be traced back to Minnesota's Scandinavian immigrants. Today, there are hundreds of cooperatives in operation in the state, including gas companies, telephone companies, grain elevators, energy suppliers, dairies, and many other kinds. More recent immigrants are also creating cooperatives, such as the Hmong American Farmers Association cooperative that bought shared farmland for Hmong farmers south of Saint Paul. Even some of the state's most successful international businesses are cooperatives rooted in serving farmer members.

Manufacturing Grain, Lumber, and Iron

Several of Minnesota's major industries rely on manufacturing natural resources into consumer products. For example, the state is home to some of the world's biggest food-processing companies. General Mills and Pillsbury started in the 1860s as flour mills on the Mississippi River. (General Mills

started as the Washburn-Crosby Company in 1866. Company president James Ford Bell merged the Washburn-Crosby Company with twenty-six other mills to form General Mills in 1928.) Land O'Lakes was founded in 1921 as a cooperative to sell butter. Hormel Foods began as a meatpacking company in 1891 and in the 1930s became famous for its canned ham (Spam). Today, these companies sell their original products, as well as hundreds of other packaged foods, throughout the world.

An early photo of the Pillsbury mill

Minnesota's forests are also important in the state's manufacturing industries. Loggers harvest trees for manufacturing paper and paper products, as well as for furniture and construction materials. Andersen Corp. is the largest manufacturer of doors and windows in the country.

Minnesota is also a leader in manufacturing many kinds of high-tech equipment. Factories turn out everything from supercomputers and computer software to the latest medical devices and supplies. Important health-care breakthroughs include blood pumps, pacemakers for damaged hearts, and hearing aids.

Mining has also been an important industry in Minnesota for more than a hundred years. At one time, high-grade iron ore accounted for most of the mining industry. However, Minnesota's iron ore deposits had little high-grade iron ore left after World War II. Mining companies then turned their attention to a low-grade ore called taconite. Taconite is shipped via truck or train to a processing plant. There it is ground into a fine powder. The iron is extracted using a magnet. Then, the iron powder is formed into marble-size pellets. The pellets are usually shipped from Duluth to steel mills along the Great Lakes or elsewhere around the world.

To this day, Minnesota remains the nation's main supplier of iron ore. Minnesota also produces granite, limestone, sandstone, sand, and gravel. Quarries in different parts of the state mine these stones for use as building and construction materials. In southeastern Minnesota, mines produce silica sand. Silica sand is used to make glass.

Service Industries

The largest number of Minnesotans work in service industries. Service industries include hospitals, schools, insurance agencies, utility companies,

This mine is located in Virginia, Minnesota.

FAST FACT

General Mills invented a puffing gun used to make cereals such as Cheerios, Kix, and Cocoa Puffs. Wet grains are put into heavy barrels, heated, and pressurized. Then, according to a *Fortune* article, a workman "pulls a trigger. The gun goes boom! and a shower of Kix or Cheerios hits the screen like hail."

transportation and shipping firms, banks and other financial institutions, government agencies, hotels, restaurants, and stores of all kinds.

Wholesale and retail sales are important to Minnesota's economy. For example, eleven thousand people work at the Mall of America. Besides selling products, the mall is part of Minnesota's tourist industry. Each year, it attracts more people than the entire population of Canada.

Visitors from out of state come for much more than just the Mall of America. Minnesota has not one but two world-class symphony orchestras. The Minnesota Orchestra and Saint Paul Chamber Orchestra draw music lovers from all over. Museums like the Minneapolis Institute of Art, the Walker Art Center, and the Minnesota Museum of American Art are crowd pleasers. The Walker Art Center even showcases over forty pieces from its collection in the Minneapolis Sculpture Garden. Another important tourist attraction is the natural beauty of the state. Minnesotans and visitors alike enjoy the state's waters, woods, and fields. More than one million fishing licenses are sold every year. There is one boat for every six people in the state. In fact, water skis were invented by a Minnesotan. Fans of winter sports love to skate, ski, snowboard, or ride across the winter landscape on snowmobiles. The first modern snowmobile was invented in Minnesota as well. Rollerblades, too, were invented in Minnesota.

Besides participating in outdoor sports, visitors and residents like to root for the state's professional sports teams. Minnesota is home to a high number of professional teams for a state of its size. Minnesota's Major League Baseball team is the Twins, named after the Twin Cities. The Twins play at a field in downtown Minneapolis called Target Field, which opened in 2010. Fans cheer on the National Football League franchise,

Today, it's a given that airplanes have "black boxes" to record flight data and noises and conversations in the cockpit. They are an essential source of information if anything goes wrong on a flight.

Flight data recorders had been around since the beginning of flight. The Wright brothers used an instrument that could record time, distance, and engine revolutions per minute. However, these early recorders couldn't survive crashes. That's the most important time to learn what happened in a plane. Organizations across the world looked for a solution.

The **indestructible** "black box" flight data recorder was invented by a University of Minnesota mechanical engineering professor named James Ryan. Ryan began working on the idea in 1946 with General Mills. General Mills had been developing equipment for the United States military during World War II. The company continued work on a flight data recorder after the war ended. Ryan's invention focused on gathering flight data including fuel usage, exhaust emissions, temperature, velocity, altitude, and rate of descent. Flight data recorders are designed to survive enormous impacts, extremely hot and cold temperatures, deep-sea pressure, and other extreme conditions. They are painted with orange heat-resistant paint. This makes a flight recorder easily visible. Flight recorders contain underwater locator beacons in case the plane crashes in water. The recorders are placed in the tail of an airplane.

Ryan applied for a patent on his device in 1953. He received approval in 1960. Airlines were initially reluctant to use Ryan's flight data recorder. Ryan lobbied to get them put in planes by law. He succeeded. Today, all commercial aircraft must have a flight recorder.

The Invention of the Flight Recorder

Flight recorders are also known as "black boxes."

Target Field

Saint Paul's Xcel Energy Center is the home of the NHL Wild.

the Minnesota Vikings, at the US Bank Stadium in downtown Minneapolis. The stadium opened in 2016. These two new stadiums became urgent needs. The roof of the Metrodome, which the teams previously shared, collapsed in 2010. A heavy snowstorm was to blame.

The Lynx are the Women's National Basketball Association team, while the men's National Basketball Association team is the Timberwolves. The Lynx are currently the most successful professional sports team in the state. They have won four WNBA Championships since 2011. Both the Lynx and the Timberwolves play at Target Center in downtown Minneapolis. Minnesota also has a professional soccer club, the Minnesota United FC. As of 2019, the team plays at Allianz Field.

In the year 2000, seven years after the Minnesota North Stars moved away, the state again got a National Hockey League team of its own, the Wild. The Wild play at the Saint Paul Xcel Energy Center. It's the only professional sports team to play in Saint Paul. There are also hundreds of recreational and school hockey teams in Minnesota.

Growth by Industry

Minnesota's unemployment rate is generally lower than the national average. This means Minnesotans are more likely to have jobs if they want them. Of the state's eleven major sectors, nine sectors grew from August 2016 to August 2017. (The eleven sectors were identified and named by the state government.) The health care and education sector grew the fastest, adding 17,280 jobs. Construction followed in second place, adding 7,247 jobs.

Renewable Energy

Renewable energy is surging in Minnesota. In 2016, 21 percent of the state's electricity was generated from renewable sources. These sources include wind, solar, water, and biomass energy.

The majority of the renewable energy in Minnesota is generated through wind power. In 2016, the state ranked sixth in total wind power generation in the nation.

The shift from coal to renewable energy creates opportunities for new businesses and new jobs in Minnesota. For example, about four thousand Minnesotans work in the wind power industry. Two of the biggest wind energy construction companies in the nation, Mortenson and Blattner Energy, are based in Minnesota.

The renewable shift also changes how existing organizations operate. For example, Minneapolis-based Xcel Energy bought more wind power than any other United States utility company for the twelfth year in a row in 2016.

Though Minnesota can be chilly in the winter, there is also a strong solar energy presence. (Solar energy generation depends on sunlight, so the solar installations still generate power on cold, sunny winter days.) The state's largest solar installation is the North Star Solar Project in Chisago County. Additionally, Minneapolis-based Target has been installing solar panels on store roofs nationwide. Target was named the top corporate solar installer in the country in 2016.

While wind and solar installations are common throughout the state, the city of Saint Cloud launched a unique renewable energy project. The city developed a way to recapture methane gas produced by the wastewater treatment process, feed it into a generator, and convert it into energy in a cutting-edge process. Currently, the wastewater facility is entirely "off the grid" (not dependent on electricity from outside sources) for portions of the year. Eventually, the city plans to store the recaptured methane. This will make the plant the first facility in the state to be entirely off the grid every day of the year.

Solar panels are just one of the exciting ways people are generating renewable energy in Minnesota.

Minnesota's state capitol building opened in 1905.

5 Government

W hen it comes to government, Minnesotans have an important claim to fame. In the 2008 presidential election, 77.8 percent of eligible voters voted. This was a higher turnout than any state in the nation. Minnesota had the highest voter turnout again in 2016.

Local Government

Many government workers serve Minnesota by helping to run the state's cities, townships, and counties. These are all different units of local government. Four out of five Minnesotans live in cities. (Interestingly, these cities take up only about 5 percent of the state's land area.) Most of Minnesota's more than eight hundred cities are small. The majority are home to between one thousand and ten thousand people. About one hundred are "charter cities," including nearly all of Minnesota's largest cities.

Charter cities can decide, within limits, the type of local government that fits their needs. They then write their own charter, or set of rules. The rest of the cities are called statutory cities. They follow the laws and guidelines that the

FAST FACT
In Minnesota, both Democrats and Republicans are invested in renewable energy. Members of both parties have a history of working together to write new laws to protect the environment. One example is the "50 by '30" bill that was written by Democrats and Republicans in 2017. The bill aimed to make the state run on 50 percent renewable energy by 2030.

Minnesota's state supreme court has chambers in the state capitol building.

The Governor's Residence

state has adopted for local governments. Most Minnesota cities are governed by an elected city council and elected mayor. But in some cities, a city manager is hired by the elected council.

The state also has 1,782 townships, a local government structure brought over from Europe. Many townships cover rural areas that have small populations and provide services such as road maintenance, volunteer fire department services, park and recreational services, wastewater treatment, and more. A typical township is governed by an elected board of three supervisors, as well as an elected township clerk and township treasurer. In townships, many important decisions are made by citizens themselves at each township's annual meeting, including taxation.

On a higher level, the state is divided into eighty-seven counties. A five- or seven-member board of commissioners manages each county. Voters elect board members to four-year terms. They also might elect a county attorney, recorder, sheriff, treasurer, and auditor for four-year terms. Along with the cities and townships, the counties provide a variety of important services to people in Minnesota.

State Government

Like the federal (national) government, Minnesota's government has three branches. The executive branch and legislative branch work together to make and pass laws. The judicial branch makes sure the laws are followed in line with the state constitution. The legislature meets at the state capitol building in downtown Saint Paul. The state supreme court sometimes meets in the capitol building as well. Other times it meets in a building next door. The governor lives in the Minnesota Governor's Residence in the historic Summit Avenue neighborhood of Saint Paul.

Executive Branch

The executive branch is headed by the governor, who is elected to a four-year term. The lieutenant governor, secretary of state, auditor, and attorney general are also elected to four-year terms. The governor supervises the state government, plans the budget, and appoints other officials to help carry out the state's programs.

Legislative Branch

The legislative branch makes the state's laws. It has two chambers: the senate and the house of representatives. The senate has 67 members. Senators are elected for four-year terms in years ending in 2 and 6, and for two-year terms in years ending in 0. This term structure was created because voter districts are redrawn every ten years after the US census is taken. This system makes sure that a senator represents the district he or she ran for election in. The house has 134 members, elected for two-year terms.

Judicial Branch

The judicial branch applies the state's laws in court cases and sometimes decides whether a law is allowed under the state constitution. At the lowest level, there are 291 district court judges who hear about 1.3 million cases a year. Their rulings can be appealed (which is a request for a judgment reversal) to the state court of appeals. There, the case will be considered by a panel of three judges (out of nineteen appellate judges total). A case can be further appealed to the state supreme court. The supreme court is the state's highest court. It has six associate justices and one chief justice. In Minnesota, all judges are elected. They serve six-year terms with mandatory retirement at age seventy.

The state house of
representatives meets
in this chamber.

The state house of representatives meets in this chamber.

From Bill to Law

A bill is a proposed new law or change in an existing law. Anyone can suggest a bill, including individuals, the governor, agencies, and more. Most bills are suggested by legislators, however. And legislators are the only people who can move an idea through the process of bill to law.

A bill must first be presented, or introduced, by its chief author from the senate or house. The chief author is the bill's sponsor. From there, it goes to a committee of the senate or house, wherever the bill's sponsor serves. After discussing the bill, committee members reject or approve it.

If the committee approves the bill, members of the whole chamber study and discuss it. Sometimes, they may change parts of the bill or add or remove parts of it. If the bill passes in the chamber where it was first proposed, it moves to the other chamber. Both chambers must pass the exact same bill before it can go to the governor. If the second chamber approves the bill but makes changes in it, the bill goes to a conference committee. During the conference committee, members from both the house of representatives and the senate work to resolve the differences. Once the conference committee reaches a compromise, the house and senate both vote on the revised bill.

Once both chambers have passed the exact same bill by a majority vote, it goes to the governor. The governor can sign the bill. In that case, it becomes law. The governor can also allow a bill to become law by taking no action on it. If the governor disagrees with the bill, he or she can veto (reject) it. The governor can also use a line-item veto. This vetoes only specific parts of a money-related bill. If the governor vetoes the bill, it goes back to the legislature. There, it can be voted on again. It can still become law—but only if it is again passed by a two-thirds vote in both the house and the senate.

Minnesota's state legislators have made new laws in many different areas, from energy and the environment to traffic, crime, education, and taxes. Many recent state laws have been meant to help consumers and safeguard people's safety and health. For example, in 2015 the government passed a law that requires landowners with waterfront property to create buffers filled with plants like prairie grasses and flowers. These plants prevent chemicals and contaminants from entering Minnesota's lakes, rivers, streams, and drainage ditches.

In 2017, the Minnesota state government demonstrated how the different branches of government balance each other. The Republican-controlled house and senate presented a tax bill that cut taxes by $650 million. The bill included funding for the Minnesota Department of Revenue's 1,300 employees. Therefore, an entire veto would have been a big problem for the department's workers and mission. Governor Mark Dayton, a Democrat, instead used line-item vetoes. He hoped this would encourage the legislature to renegotiate parts of the bill. Instead, Republican leaders sued the governor, claiming he used the line-item veto unconstitutionally, or in a way the state constitution did not allow. The Minnesota Supreme Court found the governor acted within his constitutional powers. The court ordered the legislature and the governor to work together to renegotiate the tax bill.

Mark Dayton became governor in 2011.

Minnesota's National Representation

Minnesotans elect lawmakers to represent them in the US Congress in Washington, DC. Like all other states, Minnesota has two US senators. The number of members a state sends to the US House of Representatives is based on its population. As of 2018, Minnesota had eight representatives in the House.

The Minnesota congressional delegation has an annual tradition, started by former senator Al Franken. It's called the Hotdish-Off. Each US senator and representative bakes a hotdish (casserole), and a panel of judges selects a winner. In 2017, DFL Representative Collin Peterson's "Right to Bear Arms" hotdish, featuring bear meat, took first prize. Though members of the delegation have opposing views on many issues, events like the Hotdish-Off give them a chance to step back from their political disagreements and connect on a personal level.

Land of Lakes and Dreams

Minnesotans enjoy a high quality of life. In 2017, Minnesota was ranked the happiest state in the nation. This honor was due to its high rankings in emotional and physical well-being, work environment, and community and environment. Rankings are based on personal opinions, and it's impossible to decide which state's residents are truly the happiest. However, the survey points

Collin Peterson won 2017's Hotdish-Off.

All new laws start as ideas, and anyone can have an idea. Getting involved in politics means you can make sure your ideas are heard. Because legislators are accessible online, it's easier than ever to share your ideas with them.

Get Involved Online

To find your district's legislators, simply go to http://www.gis.leg.mn/iMaps/districts. Type in your street address and press Enter or click on your location on the map of Minnesota. A list of your state and federal representatives will appear in a sidebar.

To contact your representative or learn more about them, simply click on their picture in the sidebar. You will be taken to a page with information about the representative. The

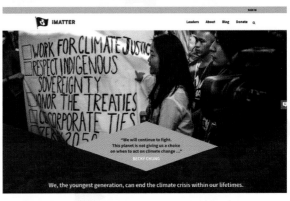

state senator and representative pages include the representative's biography, committee assignments, bills authored, news items, and contact information.

The iMatter website is a great way for young people to make their voices heard.

Your representatives are often on social media. Ask an adult to show you their social media accounts. Minnesota teens can also join iMatter. The network is made up of middle school and high school students that work toward climate change resolutions at the city level. It supports students in advocating for solutions to climate change in their communities. A group of teens presented a petition with more than 550 local student signatures to the Saint Louis Park City Council in Minnesota. In response, the council passed a Climate Inheritance Resolution. The resolution commits the city to achieving zero greenhouse gas emissions by 2040. More iMatter campaigns are under way across other Minneapolis suburbs. To learn more about iMatter, visit http://www.imatteryouth.org.

The METRO Green Line makes it easy to get around Minneapolis and Saint Paul. Minnesota's cities offer great public transportation options.

to a general truth: Minnesotans have access to excellent health care, education, and other public services. There is strong funding for the arts and many opportunities to get outside and get moving. People care about the environment and support legislation to protect it. The cost of living, even in the Twin Cities metropolitan area, is significantly lower than large cities on the coast. Yet city life in Minnesota still provides access to public transportation, a strong job market, top-notch theaters, and a bustling music scene. It might get cold in winter, but for Minnesotans, it's a small price to pay for all of the other wonderful things the state has to offer.

Glossary

abundance	A large number of something.
archaeologists	People who study past human life and activities by studying the bones, tools, etc., of ancient people.
ceded	Gave over to.
council	A group of people who are chosen to make rules, laws, or decisions about something.
custom	An action or way of behaving that is usual and traditional among the people in a particular group or place.
ecosystem	Everything that exists in a particular environment.
endangered	At risk of no longer existing as a species or group.
execution	The act of killing someone, especially as punishment for a crime.
fertile	Able to support the growth of many plants.
immigrants	People who come to a country to live there.
imported	Brought into a country to be sold.
indestructible	Unable to be destroyed.
legislature	A group of people with the power to make or change laws.
migration	The movement from one place to another.
minorities	People who are somehow different from a larger group of people, such as by race, gender, religion, or culture.
missionary	A person who is sent to a foreign country to do religious work.
plague	A huge number of insects or animals that cause damage to a place, or a disease that spreads quickly and kills many people.

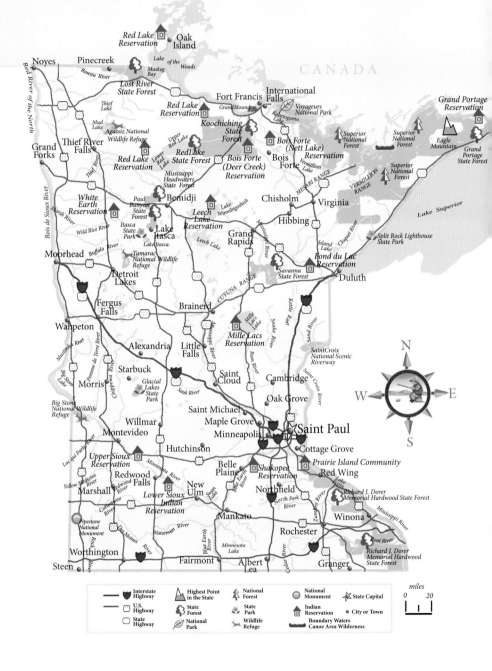

Minnesota State Map and Map Skills

Map Skills

1. To get from Noyes to Wahpeton, what highway would you take?

2. Which state forest is in the southeastern corner of the state?

3. Grand Portage is west of what lake?

4. What is the highest point in Minnesota?

5. Which direction does I-35 run?

6. To get from Fergus Falls to Brainerd, which direction would you travel?

7. What national monument is north of Steen?

8. What reservation is north of Eagle Mountain?

9. What lake is east of New Ulm?

10. What river flows through the Tamarac National Wildlife Refuge?

Answers

1. Highway 75
2. Richard J. Dorer Memorial Hardwood State Forest
3. Lake Superior
4. Eagle Mountain
5. North–south
6. East
7. Pipestone National Monument
8. Grand Portage Reservation
9. Swan Lake
10. Buffalo River

More Information

Books

Hamilton, John. *Minnesota: The North Star State.*
Minneapolis: ABDO & Daughters, 2016.

Heinrichs, Ann. *U.S.A. Travel Guides: Minnesota.* North
Mankato: The Child's World, 2017.

Whiting, Jim. *Minnesota Timberwolves.* NBA: A History of
Hoops. Mankato: The Creative Company, 2017.

Websites

Bell Museum of Natural History
https://www.bellmuseum.umn.edu
The University of Minnesota hosts the Bell Museum and
Planetarium. The museum's website features educational
resources, including a new astronomy guide each month.

Minnesota Department of Tourism
http://www.exploreminnesota.com
Learn all about Minnesota's festivals, special events, and cultural sites.

Minnesota Historical Society
http://www.mnhs.org
Explore information about Minnesota's history, look at pictures and maps,
and learn about current exhibits at twenty-six of the state's museums.

Minnesota State Legislature: Links for Youth
https://www.leg.state.mn.us/youth
The Minnesota State Legislature provides a roundup of
links for students. Browse information about how laws
are made, state representatives, and much more.

Index